DAVID'S BRAVE FLOCK

5 Bedtime Stories of Heroic Sheep

BLUME POTTER

INTRODUCTION

Imagine tucking your little ones into bed each night with stories that not only entertain but also instill timeless values of bravery, trust, and faith. David's Brave Flock: 5 Bedtime Stories of Heroic Sheep is more than just a collection of tales—it's a journey through the heart of one of the Bible's most beloved heroes, David, seen through the eyes of his faithful flock.

These enchanting stories bring to life the courage of a young shepherd who, with God's help, faces overwhelming challenges to protect his sheep. Each chapter is a gentle reminder of God's unfailing love and protection, making it the perfect bedtime read for your children or grandchildren.

As they listen to David's adventures, they'll learn important lessons about standing together in tough times, the value of each individual, and the power of faith—even in the smallest hands. This book not only nurtures their imagination but also sows seeds of spiritual growth, making it a must-have addition to your bedtime story collection.

Give your little ones the gift of courage and faith, wrapped in the warm embrace of these Bible bedtime stories. David's Brave Flock is a treasure they'll hold close to their hearts for years to come.

CHAPTER ONE:
THE PROTECTOR'S VOICE

In the rolling hills of Bethlehem, a young shepherd named David watched over his flock of sheep. The sun dipped low, casting a golden hue over the pastures, as the sheep grazed contentedly. But David knew the dangers that lurked in the shadows—the wolves that prowled, the bears that roamed, and the storms that could strike without warning.

David's sheep were not ordinary sheep; they were special, each with its own personality. There was Lily, the curious lamb who always strayed too far; Bramble, the stubborn ram who liked to challenge David's guidance; and Snowflake, the gentle ewe who cared for the younger lambs. Despite their differences, all the sheep had one thing in common—they trusted David.

David's voice was their anchor. It was strong yet soothing, a voice that brought comfort and security. "Come, my flock," David would call, and no matter where they were, the sheep would follow. They knew his voice, and they knew that as long as David was near, they were safe.

One evening, as a cold wind began to stir, the sheep sensed a storm approaching. They huddled together, their bleats filled with worry. But David was not afraid. He stood tall, his shepherd's staff in hand, and called out to them, "Do not fear, my little ones. I am here."

The sheep lifted their heads, their fear easing as they heard David's words. With a calm assurance, David led them to a sheltered cave, where they would be safe from the storm. The wind howled outside, but inside the cave, the sheep felt only warmth and protection.

As the night deepened, the sheep drifted off to sleep, comforted by the sound of David softly singing a hymn of praise to God. They knew that no matter what dangers lay ahead, David's voice would always guide them to safety. It was a voice they could trust, a voice that promised protection and love.

And so, under the watchful eye of their young shepherd, the sheep rested peacefully, knowing that they were never alone.

This was just the beginning of their many adventures with David—a shepherd who was more than just a protector; he was their leader, their friend, and their voice of hope.

CHAPTER TWO:
THE LION'S ROAR

The peaceful days in the hills of Bethlehem were not without their dangers. One afternoon, as the sun blazed high, David's sheep were scattered across the meadow, grazing happily. The air was warm, and everything seemed calm. But David's sharp eyes noticed something unusual—a rustling in the bushes at the edge of the field.

His heart quickened. He knew the signs well. There, hidden in the shadows, a pair of golden eyes gleamed. A lion, large and fierce, was crouched low, ready to pounce on his unsuspecting flock.

The sheep sensed the danger too. They bleated in fear, huddling together as the lion slowly advanced. But David did not hesitate. He stood between the lion and his sheep, his heart filled with courage, knowing that he was their protector.

With a steady hand, David reached into his pouch and pulled out a smooth stone. He placed it in his sling, swinging it with practiced ease. His eyes never left the lion, and in that moment, David prayed silently, asking God for strength.

The lion roared, a sound that echoed through the hills and sent shivers through the flock. But David did not waver. With a swift motion, he released the stone. It flew through the air, straight and true, striking the lion on the forehead.

The mighty beast staggered, then fell to the ground with a heavy thud. The sheep, who had watched in terror, now bleated with relief. Their shepherd had saved them once again.

David approached the fallen lion, his heart still racing. He knelt beside it, thanking God for giving him the courage and skill to protect his flock. The sheep gathered around him, their trust in their shepherd now stronger than ever.

That day, the flock learned a powerful lesson—that even in the face of great danger, they were never alone. David, with his unwavering faith and bravery, had shown them that courage comes from trusting in God's strength.

As the sun set, painting the sky with hues of orange and pink, David led his sheep back to the safety of their pen. The lion's roar was no longer a threat, and the sheep knew that as long as David was with them, they had nothing to fear.

And so, they settled in for the night, comforted by the presence of their brave shepherd, who had faced the lion and emerged victorious, protecting them with all the strength God had given him.

CHAPTER THREE:
THE BEAR'S ATTACK

The days passed peacefully after the encounter with the lion, but the hills of Bethlehem were full of surprises. One morning, as the sheep grazed near a cluster of trees, the calm was shattered by a loud rustling sound. The sheep froze, their ears twitching, as a large, dark shape emerged from the underbrush—a bear, massive and menacing, its eyes fixed on the flock.

The sheep began to panic, bleating in fear and scattering in all directions. But David, ever watchful, quickly called out to them, his voice strong and reassuring. "Stay close, my flock!" he commanded, and the sheep, remembering his bravery against the lion, hurried to gather around him.

The bear growled, taking slow, heavy steps toward the flock. But this time, the sheep did not run in fear. Instead, they huddled together, their eyes fixed on David, trusting that he would protect them.

David stood tall, his shepherd's staff in hand, ready to defend his sheep. He knew the bear was a fierce opponent, but he also knew that together, they were stronger. With a swift movement, David grabbed a heavy stone and loaded it into his sling.

The bear charged, but David was quicker. With a mighty swing, he released the stone, striking the bear squarely on the nose. The bear roared in pain, stumbling backward, its attack halted.

Seeing their shepherd's courage, the sheep remained close, their fear replaced by a sense of unity. Together, they watched as the bear, defeated and confused, turned and lumbered back into the forest.

David let out a deep breath, his heart pounding, but his resolve unshaken. He looked down at his flock, huddled together at his feet, and smiled. "You were brave, my little ones," he said softly. "When we stand together, nothing can harm us."

The sheep bleated in agreement, nuzzling closer to David, grateful for his protection. They had learned that in times of danger, staying close to their shepherd and to each other made them stronger.

As the sun climbed higher in the sky, David led his flock back to the safety of the pasture. The threat of the bear had passed, and the sheep knew that as long as they were united, with David as their guide, they could face any danger.

That night, as they settled down to sleep, the sheep felt a deep sense of peace. They were not just a flock; they were a community, bound together by trust and love, led by a shepherd who would always protect them, no matter what dangers came their way.

CHAPTER FOUR:
THE MISSING LAMB

It was a quiet evening in the hills of Bethlehem. The sun was setting, casting a warm glow over the pasture as David counted his sheep, ensuring each one was safe and sound. But as he neared the end of his count, David noticed something was wrong—one of the lambs was missing.

His heart skipped a beat as he scanned the flock, looking for the little lamb with the white patch on its ear. But it was nowhere to be seen. The other sheep bleated softly, sensing David's concern. He knew he couldn't rest until the lamb was found.

Without hesitation, David left the safety of the flock and set out into the growing darkness. The hills were vast, filled with hidden dangers, but David was determined. Every sheep in his care was precious, and he would not leave even one behind.

He searched through the rocky terrain, calling out the lamb's name, his voice echoing through the night. "Where are you, little one? Come to me, and I'll keep you safe."

Finally, after what felt like hours, David heard a faint bleat. He followed the sound, and there, caught in a thorny bush, was the missing lamb. Its wool was tangled, and its tiny body trembled with fear, but as soon as it saw David, the lamb's eyes brightened with recognition.

David gently freed the lamb from the thorns, cradling it in his arms. "You're safe now," he whispered, his voice full of relief and love. The lamb nestled against him, comforted by his presence.

With the lamb secure, David made his way back to the flock. As he approached, the other sheep looked up, their eyes shining with relief as they saw their lost friend return. David placed the lamb down, and it quickly rejoined the others, bleating happily.

David smiled, watching as the flock gathered around the lamb, nuzzling it with affection. "Every one of you is important," he said softly, his heart full. "I will always come for you, no matter how far you wander."

That night, as the sheep rested, they felt a deep sense of security. They knew that their shepherd loved each of them dearly and that he would go to any lengths to protect them. David had shown them that even when one was lost, they were never truly alone.

And so, under the watchful eye of their devoted shepherd, the flock slept peacefully, knowing that they were cherished, each one valued beyond measure.

CHAPTER FIVE:
THE GIANT'S FALL

The sun rose gently over the hills of Bethlehem, but this day was different from any other. David's flock could sense it. Their shepherd had left early that morning, his heart set on a mission far greater than anything they had faced before. The sheep huddled together, feeling a mix of worry and hope as they waited for his return.

They had heard whispers among the other shepherds about a giant named Goliath—a warrior so fierce that no one dared to face him. But David, their brave shepherd, had stepped forward, armed only with his faith, a sling, and five smooth stones.

The sheep knew David's strength. They had seen him defeat lions and bears, and they trusted him completely. But still, the day dragged on, and their hearts were heavy with concern. They bleated softly, their eyes fixed on the horizon, waiting for the first sign of David's return.

As the sun began to set, casting long shadows across the pasture, the sheep suddenly heard a familiar sound—the steady, confident steps of their shepherd approaching. Their hearts leaped with joy as they saw David appear over the hill, his face shining with triumph.

David had done the impossible. With a single stone, he had brought down the mighty Goliath, proving that with God's help, even the smallest and seemingly weakest could achieve great things.

The sheep gathered around David, their bleats of joy filling the air. He knelt down, running his hands through their wool, reassuring them that all was well. "We are safe, my flock," he said softly. "God has given us victory."

The sheep nuzzled closer to David, their hearts swelling with pride and love for their shepherd. They had always known that David was special, but now they saw just how strong his faith was, and how that faith had protected them all.

That night, as the stars twinkled above, the sheep slept soundly, knowing that they were in the care of a shepherd who was not only brave but also deeply faithful. David's victory over Goliath was their victory too, a reminder that with faith, anything was possible.

And so, the flock rejoiced, their hearts filled with gratitude and trust in their shepherd, who had faced a giant and returned victorious. The hills of Bethlehem were peaceful once more, under the watchful care of David, the shepherd who had led them through every danger with courage, love, and unwavering faith.

www.ingramcontent.com/pod-product-compliance
Lightning Source LLC
Chambersburg PA
CBHW081305130726
47998CB00010B/2942